The Pets at Home guide t

Goldfish

Expert advice on caring for your pet

⬩ **pets** at home™

Most modern aquariums come equipped with a hood that incorporates fluorescent lighting tubes.

© 2006 Interpet Publishing Ltd.

Published by Interpet Publishing, Vincent Lane, Dorking, Surrey RH4 3YX, England.

Hardback ISBN 13: 978-1-84286-127-1
Hardback ISBN 10: 1-84286-127-1

Paperback ISBN 13: 978-1-84286-122-6
Paperback ISBN 10: 1-84286-122-0

The information and recommendations in this book are given without any guarantees on the part of the consultant or publisher, who disclaim any liability with the use of this material.

Publishing credits
Editor: Anne McDowall
Consultant: Anna Robinson
Designed and prepress: Stuart Watkinson
Computer graphics: Stuart Watkinson
Production management: Consortium, Poslingford, Suffolk
Print production: Sino Publishing House Ltd, Hong Kong
Printed and bound in China

CONTENTS

Introducing Goldfish

Understanding where goldfish come from and how they live

Goldfish are probably the most popular pet fish in the world. A goldfish aquarium forms a decorative feature in any room. Unlike other ornaments, however, goldfish do require some care and attention – though they're much more 'low-maintenance' than most other pets. The artificial environment in which they are kept needs to be carefully set up and then needs regular cleaning and water changes to keep the water healthy and allow the fish to breathe.

The first goldfish

All goldfish belong to a single species, *Carassius auratus*, which originally came from China. Fish breeders in southern China noticed that the drab-coloured wild Carp occasionally produced fish with brighter colours, shinier scales or unusual fin shapes. Selective breeding from these natural mutations resulted in various golden forms, and later many other varieties were developed.

GOLDFISH AS PETS TIMELINE

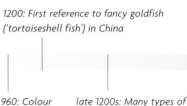

1200: First reference to fancy goldfish ('tortoiseshell fish') in China

960: Colour forms first kept as pets in China

late 1200s: Many types of goldfish kept in China, singly or in pairs, in decorative shallow bowls

WHY KEEP GOLDFISH?

More people in the world keep goldfish than any other pet. These enduringly popular fish are ideal pets for many reasons. They are:

● **inexpensive** – after the initial costs of setting up an aquarium, goldfish are cheap to maintain.

● **beautiful** – the Common goldfish is graceful and brightly coloured and there are many more 'fancy' varieties, too.

● **hardy** – Goldfish are the hardiest of aquarium fish, though fancy varieties do have some special requirements.

● **low-maintenance** – once the aquarium is properly set up, goldfish are easy to care for.

● **long-lived** – even in a small tank, goldfish can live for around 10 years.

● **stress-reducing** – fish in a well-maintained aquarium are a joy to watch and provide a great antidote to the stress of modern life.

Common goldfish are ideal fish for the new fishkeeper: not only do they look beautiful, but they are also cheap and easy to maintain.

1500s: Goldfish introduced in Japan

1700: Breeding of goldfish established in Japan and more fancy forms begin to be developed, including the Ranchu and Ryukin

1800s: Australia and New Zealand introduced to the goldfish

Late 1800s: First goldfish farm established in the USA, in Maryland

1500s: Development of some fancy varieties, including the Fantail and Veiltail

1700s: First goldfish introduced in Europe

mid 1800s: Goldfish introduced in North America

1900s: Many new fancy varieties introduced in Europe

Basic Biology – how fish 'work'

Although you may be able to describe what a goldfish looks like, many questions may remain about how it functions. What do the fins do? Why is a goldfish gold? Can it hear? Does it need to sleep? A basic understanding of how goldfish live and 'work' can also help you to care for your fish better.

Skin, scales and colour

An outermost layer of skin, the epidermis, forms a very fine coating over the fish's scales. The scales are actually transparent and beneath them lies a thin layer of skin containing pigment (colour) cells and also a layer of crystalline material called guanine. It is the guanine that creates the characteristic metallic sheen of most goldfish. (Goldfish that have a 'matt' rather than a 'gloss' appearance lack this guanine). The colour of the fish depends

The shimmering appearance of this Ranchu goldfish is produced by reflective guanine. The angle of light affects the degree and coloration of the metallic effect.

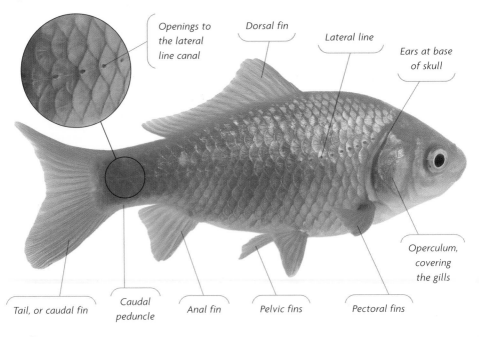

Openings to the lateral line canal

Dorsal fin

Lateral line

Ears at base of skull

Tail, or caudal fin

Caudal peduncle

Anal fin

Pelvic fins

Pectoral fins

Operculum, covering the gills

on the type and combination of pigment cells. White (silver) coloration on a goldfish occurs where there are no pigment cells at all.

How goldfish swim

Powerful muscles down either side of the goldfish's body pull the tail, or caudal fin, from side to side to provide forward movement. The other fins are used as stabilisers, steering paddles and brakes. The dorsal and anal fins stop the body from rolling sideways, while two sets of paired fins – the pectoral and pelvic fins – help with steering and stopping and also prevent the head from pitching up and down.

Fancy goldfish with unusual body shapes or fins may be handicapped in swimming. Short-bodied goldfish are low on power, while those with long fins may have steering problems.

tip *Don't touch!*
If you need to handle your goldfish, make sure you have wet hands or you will damage its fragile skin.

All the fins are at work here as the fish turns and changes its position in the water.

The caudal fin is used to provide forward movement

Short-bodied fancy varieties may have swimbladder problems because of their shape.

THE SWIMBLADDER – AIDING BUOYANCY

Goldfish have a gas-filled bag in the centre of their body called the swimbladder. Gas can be added or withdrawn from the swimbladder to allow the fish to remain buoyant at any depth. The swimbladder is connected by nerves to a series of inner ear bones in the fish's head and helps to amplify sound as well as aid balance.

Breathing and eating

Like all fish, goldfish extract oxygen from the water through their gills. They draw water in through their mouth and it passes out through the gills, inside which thread-like blood vessels near the surface take in oxygen and pass out waste carbon dioxide. If water quality is poor, there will not be enough oxygen for them to breathe.

The gills are covered by a protective shield called the operculum, whose curved shape you can see clearly behind the eye.

The gills are also used to create a partial vacuum that enables goldfish to suck up their food. Their mouths are toothless, but they have special teeth located well back in their throats to grind up food as it goes down.

The goldfish's senses

Goldfish are acutely aware of the world around them. Although they do not have external ears, their inner ears can translate underwater vibrations into clear sound. They also pick up pressure waves with their lateral line system, which connects to a series of pits along the flanks. The lateral line allows fish to sense what is happening in their immediate surroundings.

Goldfish eyes are simple in structure but they can focus on near and far objects and they also have colour vision. Except in some fancy varieties, eyes are on the sides of the head and move independently of each other.

In the wild, where visibility may be poor, fish rely on taste and touch senses to find their food. Goldfish also use sensory organs to detect chemical signals in the water.

tip Don't tap the tank!

Water is a very efficient conductor of sound waves and even a gentle tap on the aquarium glass can cause shock to your fish.

Goldfish rely as much on their senses of smell, touch and taste as on sight to locate their food, particularly where visibility is poor.

The delicate 'bubble' of the Bubble-eye goldfish is a fluid-filled pouch, or sac, that protrudes from beneath each eye.

tip **Turn off lights at night**

Goldfish do sleep at night although they can't close their eyes – they will usually sink to the bottom of the tank and their colours will fade slightly. They sleep best in the dark and need undisturbed sleep to remain healthy.

Bubble-eye goldfish need to be kept in a bare tank with no plants or ornaments on which they could damage their delicate eyes.

LIVING IN COMMUNITY

Goldfish are peaceful, community fish and happiest living with others. Buy at least two initially, then add others, but make sure that you stick to appropriate stocking levels for the size of your tank (see page 47). See chapter 2: Goldfish Varieties (pages 10–21) for more on housing different varieties together.

Comets are fast swimmers and should be kept only with other non-fancy varieties such as Shubunkins and Common goldfish.

Goldfish Varieties

Choosing the best varieties for your tanks and level of experience

Characteristics

Egg-shaped
(short fat body)

Fancy fins
(long, trailing, double fins)

Goggle eyes
(enlarged protruding eyes)

Goldfish come in more than 100 varieties. Some have the normal streamlined form while others have short, egg-shaped bodies or fins that are long and trailing, doubled, split or, in the case of the dorsal fin, absent altogether. Some goldfish varieties have unusual heads, with a fleshy hood, warty 'pompoms' on the nose, huge pouches beneath the eyes, or 'telescopic' eyes on stalks. And not all goldfish are gold – they may be white, black, brown, blue, purple or variegated.

Best for beginners

As a general rule, the nearer a goldfish is to the original, natural design, the easier it is to keep. The Common goldfish, which resembles its wild ancestor in all but colour, is the hardiest of the tribe. With no exaggeration to distract the eye from its beautiful colour and metallic sheen, it is also one of the most attractive. It is the most popular goldfish and is recommended for novice fishkeepers.

CHOOSING FANCY VARIETIES

The more a variety departs from the 'natural' goldfish shape, the more likely it is to need extra care. There are three main areas that novices should approach with caution: body shape, fin shape and eyes.

Goldfish varieties	Potential problems
e.g. Fantail, Ranchu, Lionhead	A shorter swimbladder means these fish are slower, more awkward swimmers. They're also prone to swimbladder disease. Compression of the body may also affect digestion so careful attention needs to be paid to their diet.
e.g. Oranda, Veiltail, Ryukin	Long fins are at greater risk of injury, infection and parasite infestation. Long-finned fish are slower swimmers and more sensitive to water termperature.
e.g. Globe-eye, Bubble-eye, Celestial	Goggle-eyed fish tend to be delicate. They have difficulty seeing and finding food and are prone to eye injury and infection.

tip

Don't mix varieties!

Common goldfish, Comets and Shubunkins are tougher, faster, more active and more aggressive than fancier varieties. Don't try to house the two types together or the latter may become stressed or injured and will find it hard to compete for their share of food.

The striking silver and black Panda Butterfly is a popular variety, but not one for the beginner.

Common goldfish

The 'original', single-tailed goldfish is the easiest variety for beginners to keep. Common goldfish are farm-reared for the 'pet' market; hobbyists focus on breeding high-quality specimens.

All Common goldfish are metallic but they can be self-coloured (all one colour) or variegated (a combination of colours). Self-coloured Common goldfish may be red, orange, yellow, blue, brown or black. Silver may also be included in variegated forms.

The body shape should be sturdy with a smooth outline; fins should be erect and colours bright. Patterns should be clear, balanced and extend into the fins.

The tail of the Common goldfish has short lobes which are slightly rounded at the tips.

Common goldfish are found in self-coloured forms, such as this elegant canary yellow.

These active young Sarasa Comets are constantly on the move. This is one of the most popular colours of this variety.

Comet

Comet

The Comet, which was first bred in the late 1800s in the USA, is similar to the Common goldfish except that it has a more slender body and its tail fin is longer and deeply forked.

Comets are very hardy and another ideal choice for beginners. You will need to allow them plenty of swimming space because they're also very active. One of the most popular colours is the Sarasa, which is red and silver.

Bristol Shubunkins have longer fins than London ones.

VARYING SIZES

If they're given plenty of swimming space, Common goldfish and London Shubunkins can reach 20cm (8in) or more in the aquarium. Comets are slightly smaller, while Bristol Shubunkins will rarely exceed 12cm (5in) in length.

Shubunkin

Another popular and hardy single-tailed variety, the Shubunkin is available in two forms: the London and the Bristol. The London Shubunkin is identical to the Common goldfish in body shape and finnage, while the Bristol has longer and more developed fins.

Shubunkins typically have multicoloured – calico – markings. In show-quality fish, blue should form the background colour and be present over at least 25 percent of the fish. There should also be areas of violet, red, orange, yellow and brown and an even distribution of black spots.

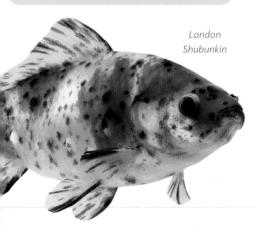

London Shubunkin

Fantail

Fantails have a deep body and a divided and forked tail fin, which is the major characteristic of the variety. All fins except the dorsal fin should be paired and have slightly rounded tips. Fantails can be metallic self-colours, variegated or calico (multicoloured).

The caudal fin on this fish is clearly fan-shaped and held erect as it swims.

Metallic Variegated Fantail

The caudal fin should be divided, forked and fan shaped.

Metallic Sarasa Fantail

Veiltail

Veiltails have a short body and a long and flowing tail fin – it should be at least three-quarters of the length of the body. The flowing fins are easily damaged, so it is best to keep Veiltails with other long-finned varieties and to avoid sharp rocks or other decorations in the aquarium. Good-quality Veiltails are difficult to breed.

Calico Ryukin

Ryukin

The Ryukin is regarded as a Japanese variety and it is very popular there. It is quite a large variety – it can grow to about 20cm (8in) – with a deep body, which slopes steeply from behind its long and distinctly pointed head. It has a high dorsal fin and long tail fin with three or four lobes. Ryukin can be self-coloured metallic, variegated or calico.

tip

Provide plenty of space

Fancy goldfish of this body shape need a tank at least 60cm (24in) long to give them adequate swimming space.

Red and White Ryukin

Oranda

This short-bodied, high-backed goldfish has long, paired fins, a high dorsal fin and a raspberry-like hood covering the head. Some Orandas also have telescope eyes. Orandas are not the easiest of goldfish to keep – they are vulnerable to swimbladder disease and fungal infections – and need a good, varied diet.

Redcap Oranda

Red Metallic Oranda

Chocolate Pompom

Pompom

The distinguishing feature of this variety are the two bunches of fleshy lobes, resembling pompoms, that have developed from the flap of skin (the nasal septum) separating the orifices forming the two nostrils on either side of the fish's head. In good-quality Pompoms these lobes are of equal size. The Pompom's body shape and arrangement of fins are similar to those of the Celestial and Bubble-Eye (see page 18).

Red Metallic Ranchu

Ranchu

This highly prized Japanese variety is very similar to the Chinese Lionhead (see below). Its main distinguishing feature is its lack of the dorsal fin. The back is steeply arched, while the tail fin, which is fully divided, faces almost downwards. It has a hood, or 'wen' covering the head. As well as metallic self-coloured and variegated forms, there are also nacreous varieties – with a dull mother-of-pearl shine – including 'sakura nishiki', which is red and white, and 'edo nishiki', which is calico.

Red and Silver Metallic Ranchu

Lionhead

Originally bred in China to resemble the mythical lion dog, the Lionhead is very similar in appearance to the Ranchu. The main difference is that its back slopes gently and smoothly towards the tail.

Pay careful attention to diet

Egg-shaped varieties like these are prone to swimbladder problems and flake foods are not suitable unless soaked (see page 51).

The hood of this Red Lionhead covers the top of its head and extends downwards and around its eyes and gill covers.

Celestial

The most obvious features of this small, twin-tailed fancy goldfish – and the ones that give it its name – are the protruding eyes on the top of its head, which gaze permanently upwards. This can make for problems with feeding if it is kept with other varieties as it may not get its fair share. Young Celestials look much like other goldfish; the eyes start to migrate around the head as the fish mature.

tip

Avoid sharp objects

House Celestials and Bubble-eyes in a relatively bare tank – and avoid strong lighting – to prevent eye injuries. These are not varieties for the beginner.

In good Celestials, the spherical protuberances around the eyes should be well developed and the same size.

Bubble-eye

Bubble-eye

The Bubble-eye has a similar body shape and arrangement of fins to the Celestial: it has a deep body, lacks the dorsal fin and its back slopes towards the caudal fin, which should be clearly divided and forked. All other fins are paired and should have rounded edges. The Bubble-eye takes its name from the extremely overdeveloped fluid-filled pouches of skin under and around the eyes.

*Calico
Globe-eye*

Globe-eye

Also known in the USA as the Telescope-
eye and in the Far East as the Dragon
Fish, this fancy variety has eyes that
protrude from the head. It has an
overall body shape similar to that
of the Veiltail (see page 15), a
single dorsal fin and other fins
are paired with pointed tips.
The caudal fin is long and
should be forked to
about a quarter of
its length.

*The protruding eyes
are clearly visible in
this view of a Calico
Globe-eye.*

*The eyes should be
symmetrical and at the
tip of truncated cone-
shaped protuberances.*

*Red-and-Black
Globe-eye*

Panda Butterfly

This variety is very similar to the Globe-eye (see page 19). Its name is derived from its coloration – black and white (silver) – and its tail, which, when viewed from above, looks like the wings of a Swallowtail butterfly. Ideally the colours should be balanced on either side of the body and the black should be intense and the silver bright. Sometimes known as the Magpie, this is a relatively new variety that is gaining in popularity.

Although mainly white, this is still a fine Panda Butterfly.

Ideally, the caudal fin of this young Panda Butterfly should be fully divided.

Black Moor

Also known as the Broadtail Moor, this variety is essentially a black Veiltail (see page 15) with globe-eyes. The coloration should be velvety black, with no bronze or silver, but perfect examples of this enduringly popular variety are hard to find and bronze scalation tends to show through on older fish.

Black moor

> *The protruding eyes should be large and spherical.*

Pearlscale

The Pearlscale is a very attractive and hardy variety. Each scale of the Pearlscale is thickened in the centre with a deposit of calcium carbonate (chalk), which makes it stand proud. Its forked and divided tail is carried high and it has an almost spherical body, a rather dainty head and small mouth.

Pearlscale

HAMA NISHIKI

The Hama Nishiki is similar to the Pearlscale, but is slightly larger and has a 'wen' (hood) like that of an Oranda (see page 16).

Setting up an Aquarium

Creating a safe and healthy home for your goldfish

Most goldfish varieties are inexpensive both to buy and to maintain – once you've properly set up their aquarium, that is. Even if you plan to keep only a few Common goldfish, you will need to budget for an adequate-sized tank, a good filtration system, lighting and tank décor. You may also want to buy a heater to maintain a constant water temperature. Choose carefully, follow the instructions and advice given on the following pages and stick to a few basic maintenance tasks (see chapter 4, pages 50–55) and your goldfish will enjoy a stress-free environment and you a stress-free hobby!

EQUIPMENT CHECKLIST

Set up the aquarium responsibly and you will avoid the problems of sick and dying fish. Make sure that you have thought about, chosen and budgeted for the following:

Lighting (see pages 35)

Does the hood have integrated light fittings or will you need to fit lighting yourself? Will you also need a condensation tray and do you want to invest in a cable tidy?

Filter (see pages 30–3)

Is it included in the tank you've selected? If not, do you opt for an external, internal or undergravel filtration system?

Tank (see pages 24–5)

What size? Bowl or tank? 'All-in-one' system or separate tank? Glass or acrylic? Do you need a stand? Does the tank have an integral hood?

Thermometer (see page 34)

Internal or digital external?

Heater (see page 34)

Do you need one?

Substrate (see pages 28–9)

Sand, gravel or pebbles? What colour? Does it need to act as a plant-growing medium?

Décor (see pages 36–7 and 42–3)

You may want to buy bogwood, rocks and other decorative items but check they are suitable for the varieties you plan to keep.

Background (see pages 42–3)

If you need/want one, what colour or design? Does it need to be added before the aquarium is filled with water?

Plants (see pages 40–1)

Real or plastic? How many? What types?

Choosing an Aquarium – bowl or tank?

Keeping goldfish has – fortunately – come a long way since the days when you brought a goldfish back from the fair in a plastic bag and tipped it into a small goldfish bowl! These old-fashioned goldfish bowls had a very narrow neck, which prevented the water from absorbing sufficient oxygen. They also had no capacity for filtration. Until recently, a rectangular tank, which could be both aerated and filtered, was the only responsible option.

Modern goldfish bowls such as this one incorporate an air pump and filtration system. This one has a capacity of 30 litres (6.6 gallons).

Modern goldfish bowls

Improvements in aquarium technology have led to the development of 'all-in-one' goldfish bowls with a built-in air pump and filtration system, thus solving the aeration and filtration problems of old-fashioned goldfish bowls.

This compact aquarium, with integrated lighting in its hood, creates a spectacular display, with real and plastic plants, despite its small size.

tip

Buy a big enough tank

Don't make the mistake of choosing an aquarium that is too small for the numbers of fish you want to keep. Buy as large a tank as you can afford and have space for.

This vertical design provides less water surface area for oxygenation than a horizontal one, so a pump is essential to aerate the water.

Glass and plastic aquariums

The most common and adaptable tank is still the long, rectangular aquarium. Other shapes are available, for example units that will fit into a corner, but tall, narrow ones are best avoided, as these offer little

An 'all-in-one' tank can often be cheaper, and it has the filter and heater already fixed in it.

swimming room for fish or surface area for oxygenation. Modern aquariums may be made from glass or acrylic. All-glass tanks are strong and easily cleaned. Acrylic tanks are virtually indestructible, though they do scratch easily, but they tend to be available only in smaller sizes. They are also more expensive than glass ones.

Aquarium hoods

A secure and ventilated cover for the tank will prevent fish leaping out and cats or children sticking their paws or hands in! It will also reduce water loss by evaporation. Many tanks now come with an integrated hood that incorporates fluorescent lighting tubes.

SIZE AND CAPACITIES OF STANDARD TANKS

Tank	Volume	Weight of water
60x30x30cm (24x12x12in)	55 litres (12 gallons)	55kg (120lbs)
60x30x38cm (24x12x15in)	68 litres (15 gallons)	68kg (150lbs)
90x30x30cm (36x12x12in)	82 litres (18 gallons)	82kg (180lbs)
90x30x38cm (36x12x15in)	104 litres (23 gallons)	104kg (230lbs)
120x30x30cm (48x12x12in)	109 litres (24 gallons)	109kg (240lbs)
120x30x38cm (48x12x15in)	136 litres (30 gallons)	136kg (300lbs)

tip

Avoid old tanks

Old tanks may be faulty, particularly if they are metal framed. If you do acquire one, though, make sure you seal joints with silicone before use and seek advice on cleaning it.

Locating the Tank – health and safety

Choosing where to place the aquarium is very important. Obviously, you will want to find a position for it where you can enjoy watching your fish on a regular basis. But you will also need to consider not only the health of the fish, but also the safety and wellbeing of your home and its occupants, particularly if you have young children.

Stands and cabinets

Once filled with water, an aquarium is very heavy (see page 25) and most domestic furniture won't be able to support its weight. It is worth investing in a purpose-built stand or cabinet, which will have the added advantages of providing a useful baseboard or shelf on which to house an external filter or other equipment and of raising the tank to a suitable viewing height.

Whether or not you use a stand, you will need to ensure that the aquarium base is completely level to prevent stress to the glass. Many aquariums come with a 'floating base', where a built-in frame supports the tank bottom, while others will need to be cushioned with a thick sheet of polystyrene.

Metal stands like this are supplied flat-packed. The black baseboard makes a useful shelf.

LOCATION CHECKLIST

Your chosen site for the tank should provide the following:
● peace and quiet for your fish
● a place away from windows, radiators and doorways
● a strong, stable floor surface
● easy access to electrical power points

Make sure that the base of the aquarium is level and secure before you begin filling it.

CHOOSING A SUITABLE LOCATION

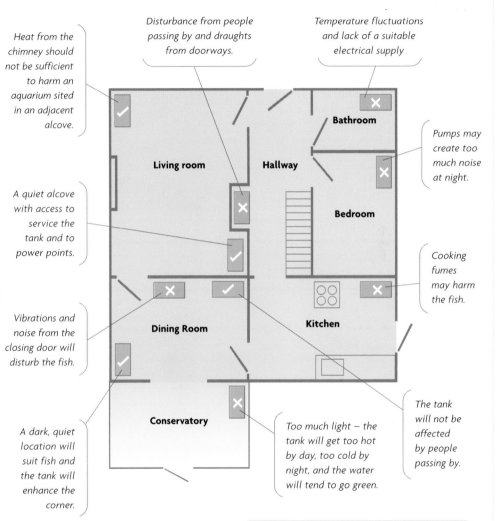

Heat from the chimney should not be sufficient to harm an aquarium sited in an adjacent alcove.

Disturbance from people passing by and draughts from doorways.

Temperature fluctuations and lack of a suitable electrical supply

Bathroom

Pumps may create too much noise at night.

Living room

Hallway

A quiet alcove with access to service the tank and to power points.

Bedroom

Cooking fumes may harm the fish.

Vibrations and noise from the closing door will disturb the fish.

Dining Room

Kitchen

A dark, quiet location will suit fish and the tank will enhance the corner.

Conservatory

Too much light – the tank will get too hot by day, too cold by night, and the water will tend to go green.

The tank will not be affected by people passing by.

tip *Check the tank is level*
Use a spirit level to check that the tank is secure and level before you fill it with water. If your stand has screw feet, get someone else to hold the tank steady while you adjust them.

CLEANING THE NEW TANK

Before you start adding anything to the new aquarium, you will need to clean the glass inside and out to remove any dust and sticky residues. You can use non-abrasive spray cleaner on the outside of the glass, but use only water and a clean cloth on the inside.

Substrates – which type to choose

Choosing sand or gravel to cover the bottom of your tank involves more than deciding what will look best. As always, you need to consider the needs of the fish and also of any plants, if you're planning to use real ones. Aquatic dealers and pet shops sell a wide range of sand and gravel – both natural and coloured and in different sizes – that is safe for aquarium use.

Adding the substrate

Even though the gravel you buy for aquarium use will be described as 'washed', it is likely to be very dusty and should be thoroughly washed in clean

Add the substrate from a jug, or using your hands, pouring it carefully onto the base of the aquarium.

water before you place it in the aquarium. How deep you layer it will depend on what type of filter you plan to install and on whether or not you are using real plants. Generally, a depth of 4–5cm (1½–2in) is ideal.

Add the substrate a bit at a time, using your hands or a plastic jug. Don't tip it from a height or you could crack the glass base of the aquarium. Slope it gently towards the back of the aquarium.

tip

Don't collect gravel

Don't be tempted to collect your own gravel from river beds or beaches – it may contain pollutants and you may disturb natural spawning sites and shelter for fish fry.

Rinse gravel thoroughly before use, stirring it until the water runs clear.

Plants will need a layer of substrate at least 5cm (2in) deep for their roots to grow into.

AQUARIUM SUBSTRATES

Type	Advantages	Disadvantages
Fine gravel	Looks good in smaller displays. Good for supporting plant growth.	May pack down if not regularly cleaned.
Medium gravel	Suitable for most aquarium sizes and filter systems.	May lodge in a small fish's throat.
Coarse gravel	Best for large tanks and can be mixed with medium gravel for a stream-bed effect.	May lodge in a fish's throat.
Black gravel	Shows off the colour of the fish.	Shows up dirt and droppings.
Coloured gravel	Decorative for a 'fantasy' style display.	Not good for creating a naturalistic environment.
Polished pebbles	Decorative.	Droppings and uneaten food can lodge between the grains.
River sand	Ideal for growing plants.	Cannot be used with undergravel filters. Tends to pack down and become stagnant. While searching for food, goldfish may churn up the sand and it can cloud the water and clog filters.

Filtration – for good water quality

It is crucial that you maintain good water quality if your goldfish are to survive. Water is a fish's life support, from which it obtains oxygen to breathe – but it is also the fish's toilet. In the confined environment of an aquarium, oxygen is quickly used up and waste products build up to poison the fish. Installing a pump and filter will help to remove waste products and maintain oxygen levels.

Why use a filter?

Filters come in different shapes and sizes but their basic function is the same. Firstly, the flow they create helps to oxygenate the water. Secondly, they trap large solid particles to keep the water clear. Thirdly, and most importantly, they remove ammonia.

Ammonia is a poisonous, invisible waste product produced by the fish and released into their water. The large surface area of the filter material (which may be gravel, foam or special pellets) is designed to encourage the growth of certain friendly bacteria. These bacteria break down the ammonia and convert it into less harmful substances, which can then be removed with regular water changes. Some filters also contain activated carbons, which can remove traces of chemicals, such as fish medications, from the water.

Undergravel filters

The base plate of an undergravel filter has slits and holes cut into the plastic, and is raised above the floor of the tank, creating a small gap. This plate must be installed first, then the tube known as the uplift tube, and finally, the gravel can be spread on top. (It will need to be about 6cm/2½in deep.)

The undergravel filter works by drawing water through holes in the plate and up the tube and spilling back into the aquarium at the top. The water is moved through the gravel, plate and uplift tube by means of either an airstone, connected by airline to an airpump, or by an electric water pump called a powerhead.

THE NITROGEN CYCLE

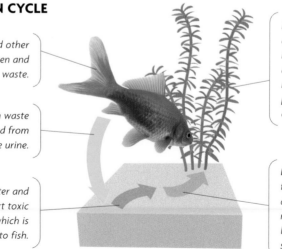

Fish eat plants and other foods containing nitrogen and excrete nitrogenous waste.

Ammonia is the main waste product and is excreted from the gills and in the urine.

Bacteria living in the filter and the substrate convert toxic ammonia to nitrite, which is still poisonous to fish.

Plants use ammonia and nitrates as food and incorporate nitrogen into proteins that are eaten by fish.

Different bacteria feed on nitrite and produce nitrate, a much less harmful substance.

Rising bubbles from the airstone oxygenate the water.

The base plate and uplift tube of an undergravel filter. A powerhead draws water up the tube.

AQUARIUM FILTRATION SYSTEMS

Type of filter	Advantages	Disadvantages
Undergravel filter	Probably the best option for bowls and small tanks.	Organic waste is retained in the tank and must be regularly removed. Plants do not thrive where undergravel filtration is used because of the constant flow of water around their roots.
External filter	Efficient, offering a large volume of media to deal with waste generated by goldfish. Saves precious space within the aquarium. Easy to access for maintenance. The best choice for large tanks.	Fins of fancy varieties may be damaged as water is sucked up the filter's intake pipes. It is quite bulky (though can be stored on a shelf or in a cabinet below the tank).
Internal filter	Ideal for medium-sized tanks, particularly if you use two filters, one at either end of the tank.	Takes up valuable tank space, particularly if you install a double internal filter system.

External and internal filters

An external power filter works by drawing water though the various media and pumping it back into the aquarium. It accommodates more media for bacteria to colonize.

An internal filter works in much the same way but operates inside the aquarium. An ideal set-up for a medium-sized aquarium is to use two internal power filters, each able to cope with a tank just over half the size of yours. Place one at either end of the tank and clean one of the filters every two weeks, or as needed.

An internal filter attaches to the inside of the aquarium. It must be under water before you switch it on.

FILTER MEDIA

Filter wool *sandwiches activated carbon*

Carbon *can be kept in a bag formed from a pair of tights, tied with a loose knot.*

Use only branded aquarium filter wool

Pelleted biomedia *support good bacteria*

A coarse foam pad *traps large dirt particles*

SETTING UP AN EXTERNAL FILTER

Pass the intake pipe through the aperture at the rear corner of the tank. Place it at the opposite end of the tank from the return pipe to create a good flow.

Allow a free flow of air around the filter. Cut the inlet and return pipes to a suitable length to keep them tidy.

SAFETY FIRST

Water and electricity make a dangerous combination. Make sure that you keep wires from the heater, pump, lighting, etc. tucked safely out of the way. Invest in a cable tidy and, more importantly, make sure that you have fitted a circuit breaker to cut off the power if there is an accident. Always switch off power before handling electrical equipment and never touch equipment or switches with wet hands.

To deliver aerated water back to the tank, use a multi-directional jet. Position this so that the flow is at, just above or just below the water surface.

Screw the taps onto the inlet and outlet ports of the motor housing. Make final adjustments with the filter in position.

Heating and Lighting

Although heating a coldwater aquarium may seem unnecessary, providing a heater in the goldfish aquarium will enable you to maintain a constant temperature, which is very important for the health and wellbeing of your fish as well as for any natural plants you may have. The right lighting will enable you to view your fish to their best advantage and will also encourage real plants to flourish.

Installing a heater

A stable temperature may be provided in a centrally heated house during the day, but at night, heating thermostats·are often turned down, leading to a fluctuation in the aquarium temperature. The optimum temperature for a goldfish aquarium is about 18°C (64°F).

Combined electronic heater/thermostats are housed inside the tank. A 100-watt model will be quite adequate for a 60cm (24in) aquarium. Install the unit at an angle, so that the rising heat does not directly pass the thermostat. The sensor should sample the ambient aquarium temperature, not a localised hotspot. Leave a gap between the bottom of the heater and the substrate.

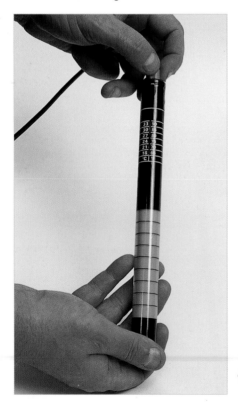

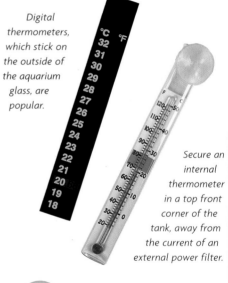

Digital thermometers, which stick on the outside of the aquarium glass, are popular.

Secure an internal thermometer in a top front corner of the tank, away from the current of an external power filter.

 Keep the heater underwater

Never turn on the heater unless the tank is filled and the water level reaches the minimum level specified on the unit.

Combined electronic heater/thermostats like this are housed inside the aquarium.

Lighting the aquarium

Fluorescent tubes are the most popular form of aquarium lighting: they are very efficient, use little electricity and are relatively cheap when used in small numbers. They are also cool, which means that they don't heat up the water as ordinary bulbs would do.

Most modern aquariums are supplied with hoods with lighting already installed and it is simply a matter of plugging the system into the electrical supply. If you want to fit lights yourself, remember that lamp fittings must be shielded from condensation and splashes.

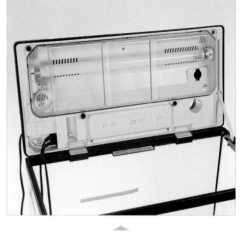

This aquarium, like most modern ones, comes with its own hood, which has fluorescent tubes incorporated within it.

This custom-built hood has an integral light fitting and a condensation tray to protect the light tube from splashes.

tip *Change tubes regularly*

To maintain optimum lighting levels in your aquarium, it is a good idea to change fluorescent tubes once a year.

Rocks and Wood – for a natural setting

The goldfish's wild cousins live near the bottom of slow-moving rivers. Creating a natural-looking environment in which your fish can live is one of the many joys of fishkeeping. Aquarist suppliers and pet shops stock pieces of rock and wood that are suitable for aquarium use and that will help make your aquarium a beautiful and interesting setting for your goldfish.

RESPONSIBLE USE OF MATERIALS IN THE TANK

• Use only materials purchased from a reputable aquarium retailer. (Don't collect them from the wild.)
• Wash materials thoroughly in warm water before adding them to the aquarium. (Avoid detergents.)
• Check that the materials you have chosen are suitable for the goldfish varieties that you wish to keep (and that there are no sharp edges).
• Avoid rock falls by securing pieces with silicone.
• Avoid calcareous rocks. (Test by dripping vinegar onto the rock – if it fizzes, don't use it.)
• Make sure that décor does not touch the heater or filter equipment.

Hand-carved 'rainbow rock'

Granite is safe, but rather stark

Westmorland rock is fairly inert unless water is very acidic

Most aquatic shops sell pebbles and boulders

Use slate to shield the sides of the tank

Scattered slate pebbles can look very effective

Sandstone chunks have a warm brown colour

Chunk of artificial lava rock

Cracks in
natural
bogwood
can double
as planting
pockets

Mopani wood has a
dark and a pale side

ADDING ROCKS AND WOOD IN THE AQUARIUM

1 Start by adding large pieces of bogwood at the rear and sides of the tank. Do not allow any décor to touch the heater or filter equipment.

2 Begin to incorporate larger rocks at the back and sides of the display. Visually, groups of odd numbers are more pleasing than even numbers.

3 Place medium-sized and smaller pieces of rock near the front of the tank. Part-bury them in the substrate – as they would be in the wild.

4 Don't overdo the arrangement of rocks and wood – you will need to allow enough space for plants too, which you will add after the water (see pages 42–3).

Water – adding and testing it

Unlike some other aquarium fish, goldfish are adaptable to variations in water chemistry and tolerant of a wide range of pH (water acidity) and hardness levels. Nevertheless, poor water quality is the biggest cause of fish health care problems, so it is important that you take the necessary steps to treat and test the water you are going to use to fill the aquarium. (Adequate filtration and routine water changes are also essential – see pages 30–3 and 52 respectively.)

Treating water ready for use

Goldfish will generally be perfectly happy with your local tapwater, but you will need to treat it first. Leaving water in clean containers (ideally with an airstone bubbling) will dissipate the chlorine, but does not deal with the problem of chloramine (chlorine with ammonia added to stabilise it while it removes harmful

Dechlorinators that remove chlorine and chloramine from tapwater are widely available and effective. Follow the instructions supplied.

bacteria from your drinking water supply). A tapwater filter can be used to prefilter your tapwater, but it must be one that is suitable for use in fishkeeping – most domestic tapwater filters are not. Most fishkeepers use a bottled chemical dechlorinator when preparing fresh water for an aquarium. Such products are available from any aquarium retailer.

Adding water to the tank

Place a small saucer on the substrate and pour the treated water from a jug onto the saucer to avoid disturbing the substrate. Continue to add water until the tank is about half full. This is the stage at which you can add plants (see pages 40–1) and fill in any gaps with other décor (see pages 42–3) if you wish. You can then add the rest of the water. If you are using an internal power filter, this should be the last item you install.

tip

Avoid rainwater and distilled or purified water

Rainwater may contain pollutants and distilled or purified water, while they may seem ideal, lack any minerals and are therefore also unsuitable for aquarium use.

Pour water slowly onto a plate on the base of the tank to avoid disturbing the substrate.

Test kits, like this one for testing nitrite levels, are easy to use.

Good water quality is vital if your goldfish are to remain healthy.

Testing the water

Once you've set up the tank and filled it with water, you can check the water quality with a series of tests for ammonia, nitrites and pH level. Test kits are simple to use and are available from all aquarist suppliers. These tests should be performed on a regular basis to monitor the water quality in your aquarium (see also Routine Maintenance, pages 52–5).

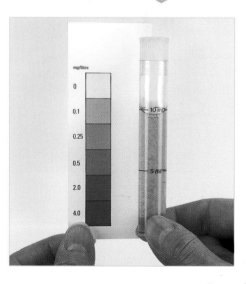

Aquarium Plants – creating a display

A goldfish aquarium in a centrally heated room rarely falls below 18°C (64°F) and will support many plant species sold for tropical aquariums. Choose healthy plants with strong root systems that will establish in the substrate and feed them weekly with a small amount of aquarium plant food.

When building up a planted display, use larger plants at the back and sides of the aquarium to create a framework. Turn each plant until you find its most pleasing 'face'. Continue planting towards the front of the tank, using smaller species to allow swimming room for the fish.

SUITABLE SPECIES

Many of these aquatic plants are sold alongside tropical plants and also do well in warmer water.

Green milfoil
Myriophyllum hippuroides

Broadleaf ludwigia
Ludwigia palustris

Spadeleaf plant
Gymnocoronis spilanthoides

Straight vallis
Vallisneria spiralis

Elodea
Egeria densa

Crispus
Potamogeton crispus

Whorled umbrella plant
Hydrocotyle verticillata

Dwarf hairgrass
Eleocharis parvula

Creeping Jenny
Lysimachia nummularia

Spatterdock
Nuphar japonica

Giant sagittaria
Sagittaria platyphylla

PLANTING LUDWIGIA FOR A STUNNING DISPLAY OF GREEN

1 Slide the plants, embedded in rockwool, out of the pot. Carefully unravel the rockwool. There may be up to three plants in each piece.

tip *Weigh down the plants*

You can prevent goldfish from digging up plant roots by placing a few small pebbles around the base of each plant to keep it weighted down.

PLASTIC PLANTS FOR EASY CARE

Real plants look great, but they do need a certain amount of care. In addition, goldfish are prone to dig around or snack on them. Plastic plants can provide an ideal solution: they are virtually everlasting and, like real plants, provide shelter and a spawning medium for fish. Their leaves and stems will be colonised by the same bacteria that live in the filter. However, because they do not take up nitrates, as real plants do, you will need to pay extra attention to water changes. Initially, even the most realistic replicas can look 'too good to be true', but as their leaves acquire a fine algae coating, their colours will tone down.

2 Create a hole in the substrate with your fingers and hold it open.

3 Put in the plant and cover the roots with substrate. Firm in gently.

4 Put in plants 2.5–5cm (1–2in) apart or leave room so that the tips of the leaves on separate plants just touch.

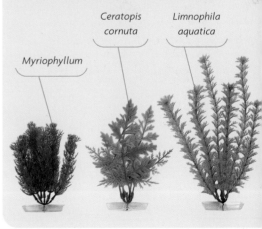

Myriophyllum

Ceratopis cornuta

Limnophila aquatica

Completing the Display – other décor

In addition to the substrate, rocks and bogwood and real or artificial plants, aquarium retailers sell a whole range of other tank décor that you might want to consider for your tank, some of which is particularly good for junior fishkeepers.

As a final touch, you will probably want to add a background to the tank. Apart from helping to create an effective display in the aquarium, backgrounds will hide the electrical cables, filter pipework and the wall behind the tank.

Choosing a background

Like the range of tank décor, backgrounds vary in style from plain black – a safe choice that will look good in any tank – to natural-looking scenes of tree roots, rocks or plants, which will give the tank a more 3-D look, to more fantastic landscapes, such as Classical temples and sunken cities. These backgrounds are usually made of plastic and sold off the roll or to an approximate size and are easy to trim with scissors. You can also buy a range of solid textured panels for the back of the aquarium, but these should be placed into the tank right at the start.

Other tank decorations

Children, in particular, will enjoy adding other decorations to the tank and provided you don't overfill the aquarium, they can help to promote an interest in fishkeeping in the very young. As with other aquarium décor, make sure that you buy only items recommended for aquarium use. Aquarium retailers stock a wide variety of items that are suitable.

Aquarium backgrounds include designs with rocks and plants. Make sure your aquarium display features these elements too.

This rock design gives a realistic 3-D feel to the finished aquarium and can be trimmed top or bottom without spoiling the result.

Novelty ornaments for the aquarium include such fantastic items as this Mr. Scary Shark, whose two halves separate to fix on the inside and outside of the tank.

MATURING THE TANK

Once the water has been added, it's tempting to go straight to your retailer and buy the fish – after all that's what all your hard work has been for. Don't! The filtration system will take up to six weeks to mature biologically, and the fish must be added gradually. If you have real plants, these will also need time for their roots to establish without disruption. Leave the aquarium lights on for 10–14 hours a day to promote their growth. Once the aquarium has been running for at least a week, you can add your first fish.

43

Buying Fish – choosing the right ones

Before buying goldfish, check out a few aquatic dealers. (If you can, take along an experienced hobbyist friend.) Look at their tanks and question staff. The goldfish you see should look healthy and alert, tanks should be clean and the water clear. Staff should be prepared to help you and be able to answer any questions you have about caring for goldfish. (Be aware, however, that staff may not have so much time to discuss your needs or answer questions on busy weekends.)

Choosing a healthy fish

Look at the goldfish in the retailer's tanks carefully. If you are buying the first goldfish for a new aquarium, choose small ones. They should be lively, interested in their surroundings and swimming freely and without effort. Avoid any that are gulping at the surface, that have splits in the fins or red or white spots on the body, which might indicate an infection.

Well-presented tanks are a good sign of a caring dealer. Here, children can see their future pets and choose them easily.

CHOOSING A FISH

Check for a good body shape with no wasting, hollowness or bloating

Colours should be clear

Don't buy too many fish

Don't be tempted to buy more than a couple of small goldfish in the first instance. Keep checking water quality and if all is going well, you can add more in a couple of weeks.

Make sure that there are no damaged scales

The fins should be erect and not clamped. Check for any splits or damage to them.

tip

Go straight home

Don't stop off on the way home; the less time the goldfish spend in transit, the better they will cope with the stress of moving.

The plastic bag in which the dealer puts your new goldfish should be inflated with air and securely sealed with a rubber band.

Taking your goldfish home

The dealer will put your chosen goldfish into a large plastic bag half-filled with water from the tank in which they've been kept and will inflate it with air and seal it with a rubber band. Ask the dealer to tape up the corners of the bag so that small goldfish cannot become trapped and damage themselves.

To keep the occupants calm on the journey home, place this bag into a brown paper bag or black plastic bin liner. Ideally, stand the bag upright inside an insulated polystyrene box and hold it in place with balls of scrunched up newspaper. This will help prevent the goldfish becoming too hot or cold.

Keeping your newly purchased goldfish in the dark will help them to stay calm during the journey home.

Adding Fish – the first few days

However well you have chosen your new goldfish, and however carefully you have transported them home, they will be stressed by the journey and will need some time to acclimatise to their new surroundings. Don't simply tip them into the new tank. The immediate environment in which the fish live — their water — will be different in the bag and in the aquarium, and you will need to make sure that the temperatures have equalised first.

The Redcap Oranda is a beautiful fish but not a good choice for new fishkeepers.

ADDING FISH TO THE AQUARIUM

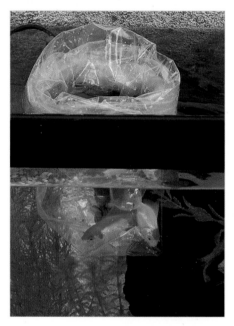

2 After 15 minutes, add some aquarium water to the bag. Leave the bag floating in the aquarium for a further 15 minutes before you gently release the new fish into the aquarium. Turn the bag on its side and hold it open with one hand. Gently tip it up with your other hand so that the goldfish swim out into the aquarium. Check that none is trapped inside the collar of the bag.

1 Turn the aquarium lights off. Take the plastic bag containing the goldfish out of the paper bag or bin liner and roll down the sides to form a collar. Carefully float the bag in the tank to equalise the temperatures between the water in which the goldfish have been transported and that in the aquarium.

Don't feed immediately

It's tempting to want to feed your new fish straight away, but heavy feeding will only overload the new filtration system. Wait until the following day and then provide only a very small amount of flake or tablet food.

3 Leave the fish to settle in their new home for an hour before you turn the aquarium lights on. The fish will probably try to hide until they become more confident. Be patient and don't try to tempt them out with food. Wait at least a week before adding more fish.

STOCKING THE AQUARIUM

It is vital not to exceed the stocking capacity for the aquarium size. The recommended stocking level for a goldfish aquarium is 60cm^2 of water surface area for each 1cm of fish length, excluding the tail. So an aquarium measuring 60 x 30 x 30cm has a surface area of 1800cm^2 and this divided by 60cm2 means that it can hold a total of about 30cm of fish. (A 24 x 12 x 12in tank can hold 12in of fish.) For an aquarium this size you could buy, for example, either 12 fish of 2.5cm (1in), and move some to other tanks as they grow, or two goldfish of 15cm (6in). However, remember that this is only a guide. Water testing can tell you if your tank is overstocked.

Caring for Your Goldfish

Enjoying your goldfish and keeping them healthy

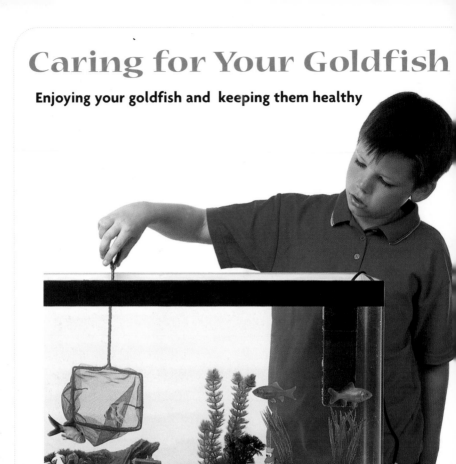

Goldfish are among the easiest fish to maintain, but their environment is crucial to their health. Making sure that the water quality in their aquarium is good is of even greater importance than feeding them regularly. (Indeed, overfeeding fish is more likely to be a problem than underfeeding them.) Establishing regular maintenance checks and routines is important if your fish and plants – if you have real ones – are to thrive. Of course, even with such attention, you may still run into problems, so make sure you learn to spot early warning signs, know where to get expert advice and take prompt remedial action.

Establishing a community

Once your initial goldfish have had a few weeks to settle in, you can begin to add more fish.

Goldfish are a shoaling species and so ideally should be kept in groups of at least six. Make sure that your aquarium is large enough to accommodate them, though, and don't forget that if you have bought small fish, they will grow. It is a good idea to buy only a couple of fish at a time, then wait for a fortnight before adding another two. If possible, do a water test for ammonia or nitrite before buying any more fish – this will tell you if your filter is coping with those you already have. If you detect either of these substances, you will need to wait until they have gone before continuing to add fish.

SAFETY IN THE AQUARIUM

Hopefully you have already chosen a site for your aquarium away from draughts, heaters, direct sunlight and cooking fumes. But as you continue to enjoy your goldfish aquarium, you will need to bear in mind some other safety factors too:

● Never use spray cans – furniture polish, hair spray, air fresheners etc – near the aquarium

● Never bang on the side of the tank as doing so will send shock waves through the aquarium.

● If you need to catch a particular fish (for example to isolate it in a quarantine tank), scoop it up carefully in a fishing net.

● Always replace the aquarium hood to prevent anything falling in (or other pets trying to scoop the fish out).

● Wash your hands after touching the tank water and do not immerse open cuts.

● Make sure that the heater is turned off before you reduce water levels in the tank.

Wait at least a week, and test the water, before adding more fish to a new aquarium.

Feeding – for good health and colour

Your goldfish are entirely dependent on you for their food and you should offer it to them regularly and in a varied form. Commercially manufactured foods contain all the essential nutrients and vitamins to keep goldfish fit and healthy.

It is best to feed goldfish a pinch at a time, offering them as much as they will eat in two or three minutes on a twice-daily basis. Initially, healthy goldfish are very keen to feed and will greedily eat the food being offered. As they consume it, however, they will gradually become less active and this is the point at which to stop feeding. This will avoid overfeeding and the problems of polluting the aquarium.

The basic diet

Flake foods are probably the most common type of manufactured diet for aquarium fish, but you can also buy pellets and foodsticks for larger fish. Always gauge the size of food you offer your goldfish on the basis of the smallest ones to ensure that they all get sufficient to eat.

A SELECTION OF DRIED AND PELLETED FOODS

Freeze-dried bloodworm *are also readily available in frozen form.*

Stick-on tablets *fix to the aquarium glass.*

Freeze-dried tubifex cubes *are safe for use in the aquarium.*

Sinking granule *provide food at substrate level.*

Proprietary flake food *can be crumbled to suit small goldfish.*

These Common goldfish have just been fed and are rising to the surface to eat the flakes.

FEEDING FANCY GOLDFISH

Short-bodied (egg-shaped) goldfish may need extra care with feeding. They are prone to buoyancy problems and floating foods can cause a problem if the fish gulp air when feeding. It pays to soak their food for a minute or so beforehand so that it sinks below the surface. Avoid soaking food for longer than this though, otherwise water-soluble vitamins such as asorbic acid (vitamin C) will begin to leach out. Some types of fish food are not suitable for soaking and will disintegrate.

Treat foods

In addition to proprietary diets, goldfish appreciate the occasional treat food. Manufactured treat foods are available in tablet form. Natural foods are always popular and very good for getting adult goldfish into breeding condition.

Frozen foods, such as bloodworm, chopped mussels and brineshrimp, are very beneficial to fish. Always thaw them out first, then give them to the fishstraight away. Never try catching your own from a local pond as they may introduce disease.

You can also offer your goldfish pieces of orange and lettuce leaves to browse on, but remove any uneaten food before it can pollute the water.

Goldfish will enjoy the occasional treat food, such as freeze-dried bloodworm.

Don't overfeed

Overfed goldfish can produce more waste than the filtration system can handle, while leftover foods will foul the water further. Poor water quality leads to health problems.

Routine Aquarium Maintainance

In order to keep your goldfish and their environment looking their best – and, more importantly – in good health, you will need to establish some daily and weekly routines. In addition, you'll need to 'spring clean' the aquarium thoroughly once a year.

A small net will enable you to catch and isolate fish for treatment

Use a gravel cleaner to suck up debris that has accumulated on the tank floor

Partial water changes

One of the most important things you can do for your goldfish is to ensure that the quality of the water in their aquarium is good. This means not only providing an adequate and fully functioning filtration system (see pages 30–3), but also siphoning out 10–20% of their water every week and replacing it with fresh. Don't use water straight from the tap: fill a bucket and leave it overnight to reach room temperature, then add a water conditioner to remove any chlorine.

Change 10–20% of the aquarium water every week.

The two halves of a magnetic cleaner stick together through the glass.

An algae scrubber has an abrasive surface to remove algae from the aquarium glass

tip Don't change too much water

Sudden changes to water chemistry can be as dangerous to the fish as neglecting the water so make sure you make partial water changes (10–20%) regularly, rather than more than this at irregular intervals.

REGULAR MAINTENANCE TASKS

Daily

- Feed goldfish a small quantity of food twice a day, removing any uneaten food after two to three minutes.
- Observe the fish closely for any signs of ill health.
- Check the water temperature.
- Check that all equipment (filters, lights, airpump and heater) is working properly.

Weekly/Fortnightly

- Make a partial (10–20%) water change.
- Test water for nitrite and pH levels. (If either of these show a problem, perform a full range of water tests.)
- Clean the glass on the front of the tank, and the sides if you wish.
- Feed aquarium plants and remove any dead plant matter.
- Use a gravel cleaner to vacuum the aquarium substrate.
- Clean cover glass or condensation tray.

Vacuum the aquarium gravel using a gravel cleaner every week or two.

Monthly/as required

- Clean the filter and replace expendable media if necessary.

Every 6–12 months

- Test water for nitrate levels.
- Service the airpump and filter/powerhead motors.
- Replace lighting tubes.
- Replace airstones and airline.
- Scrub rocks, bogwood and any plastic plants to remove build-up of algae.

Scrub aquarium décor – bogwood, rocks and plastic plants – using clean water only.

CLEANING AN EXTERNAL FILTER

1 Turn the coupling taps to the 'off' position and undo the plastic nuts securing the taps to the filter body. Place the filter in a shallow bowl and tilt it to drain off most of the water.

2 Remove the motor from the canister by releasing the locking tabs and separating the two main components. Remove the impeller and clean all plastic parts with a cloth.

3 Remove the internal basket containing the filter media. (This filter has a one-piece assembly, but some filters have separate modules for the different filter materials.)

4 Remove the filter media from the internal basket. Discard the soiled filter floss and the exhausted activated carbon. Both will need to be replaced. Gently wash the permanent media in water taken from the tank. Loose-fill the special bag, or an old stocking, with fresh carbon and reassemble the media. Replace the motor unit. Couple the filter to the taps and turn them to the 'on' position.

Keeping records

Making a note of when you carry out routine maintenance tasks and the results of water tests is a wise habit to develop. This will show you when such tasks are due and will also draw attention to any potential problems. Also note changes in behaviour of your fish, which might indicate the start of health problem.

Testing water

Until the tank is six weeks old, check for ammonia and nitrite at least once a week (or before adding more fish). Water quality problems can still arise later if the tank beomes overstocked, equipment stops working properly or you fail to carry out water changes. Check nitrite, nitrate and pH levels regularly. If you detect a problem, do a partial water change to dilute it, then consider the cause.

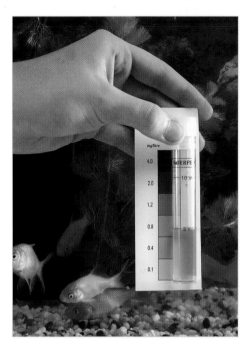

GOING ON HOLIDAY

If you are going away for only a day or two, your goldfish won't miss you. You can buy 'vacation blocks', which contain food in a compressed block that gradually dissolves in the aquarium. The best option, however, is to find a responsible friend to look after your goldfish for you while you are away, ideally in your own home. Alternatively, if you have only a couple of fish, you could move them into a smaller holiday tank to take to a friend's house, but make sure this tank has adequate filtration. Don't forget to give your friend written instructions on caring for your fish while you are away and leave the phone number of the veterinarian or local aquatic dealer or pet shop in case there are any problems. It is also a good idea to measure out the food into separate plastic bags to prevent an enthusiastic friend from overfeeding your fish.

A small holiday tank will provide a satisfactory home for a couple of goldfish for short periods of time providing it has adequate filtration.

Health Care – symptoms and cures

There will be times when, even though you have carried out all the maintenance tasks outlined on the preceding pages and done all you can to care for your fish, one or more of them may become sick. If you regularly observe your fish – through the glass rather than by netting them, which will cause them undue stress – you will soon notice when one of them starts to display unusual symptoms.

discoloration of the skin. Are your goldfish behaving differently? A sick goldfish may be more or less active than normal, may refuse to feed, and may float, sink, whirl or swim sideways. You may also notice that fins are clamped tightly to the body or that the fish scratch themselves against objects in the aquarium.

A cyst or tumour is common, but will not spread to others or impair the affected fish.

Symptoms to look for

Never ignore changes in a fish's appearance: look out for damage to skin and fins, sudden bloating, sticky faeces trailing from the vent, and spots, sores or

SPOTTING HEALTH PROBLEMS

White pimples on the skin are clear signs of white spot, a parasitic condition. (But if spots are confined to the head and gill covers, it may be a male goldfish in breeding condition.)

tip *Don't stress your fish!*
Most fish health problems are attributable to poor water quality. If water quality is poor, fish become stressed and are then susceptible to all sorts of secondary conditions.

Ulcers or red patches on the skin are caused by bacterial infections.

Scales that protrude from the body surface like a pinecone are symptomatic of dropsy.

Ragged fins may indicate damage or be symptoms of a bacterial disease called fin rot.

DIAGNOSING AND TREATING HEALTH PROBLEMS

Symptoms	Likely causes	Treatment
Pinhead-sized white spots over body, skin and fins	Whitespot: an infectious parasitic illness	Over-the-counter whitespot remedy
Whitish, fluffy blobs, anywhere on the body or fins	Fungal infection caused by physical injury or severe stress	Over-the-counter fungal remedy
Pale, slimy skin	Poor water conditions or parasitic infection, usually as a result of stress	Test water conditions. If these are good, try an external parasite remedy or consult a veterinarian.
Ragged, pale or bloody fins	Fin rot: a bacterial infection following physical injury or stress	Fin rot remedy for mild cases. In severe cases, consult a veterinarian.
Rapid, heavy breathing	Respiratory infection or very poor water conditions	Test water quality and oxygen levels. If there is no problem with these, consult a veterinarian.
Thin, sunken belly or swollen belly, protruding scales and eyes, bloodshot skin, ulcers	Serious bacterial infection, often related to severe stress	Minor ulcers may respond to antibacterial remedies. In more severe cases, consult a veterinarian.
One or more large parasites on the body (wormlike or round, usually grey or brown)	Multicellular parasites: fish lice, anchor worms or leeches	Difficult to eradicate: consult a veterinarian.
Cloudy eyes	If just one eye, physical injury. If both, poor water conditions or diet.	Usually no treatment required if the original cause is dealt with.
Abnormal tendency to float, sink or lie on one side (but otherwise healthy)	Swimbladder problems: causes are disputed but some fancy varieties are prone to this.	Maintain perfect water conditions and feed a varied diet. If problems persist, consult a veterinarian.
Missing gill covers or eyes, kinked spine, absent or misshapen fins	Usually congenital deformity. (But remember that missing dorsal fins, humped backs etc are normal for some fancy varieties.)	None. Do not breed from these individuals.

Seeking advice

If you are concerned about the health of your fish, don't hesitate to seek help. A good pet shop or aquatic dealer may be able to offer advice and they will stock a range of treatments. However, it is important that you accurately diagnose the problem so that you can administer the correct medication rather than trying several different treatments. If you are not sure what to do, always seek professional advice from a veterinarian.

Treating sick fish

When using any medication, be sure to follow the directions exactly and measure the dosage carefully. Some of these medications are very potent and an overdose could be fatal. Some medications may be administered to the

Diluting medication before adding it to the aquarium reduces the risk of producing localised spots of high concentrations.

It is worth investing in a small plastic carrying tank that can be used to take a goldfish to the veterinarian.

whole tank and will not harm other fish; in other cases you will need to isolate the sick fish in a quarantine tank. Again, follow the directions, and the advice of your veterinarian, precisely. Remember to keep any utensils in which you mix the medication solely for aquarium use and to wash them thoroughly with warm water after use.

THE QUARANTINE TANK

Use an internal filter to control fish waste and maintain water quality. Keep the water temperature constant with a heater set to 18°C (64°F).

A single plastic plant is easy to keep clean and will help the fish feel at home.

Provide a hiding place such as a piece of pipe to provide the fish with reassurance.

Screen the back and sides of the tank and avoid lighting to create a dark and tranquil environment for sick fish.

EUTHANASIA

Sometimes it is kinder to euthanase a very sick fish than to allow it to suffer. Euthanasing fish can be a complex subject and requires experience, so the best thing to do is to consult a knowledgeable aquatic retailer or, better still, a veterinarian.

Never euthanase a fish by putting it into the freezer, leaving it out of water or flushing it down the toilet, as all these methods cause unacceptable suffering. Flushing pet fish down the toilet can also pass on diseases to wild fish populations. Bury dead individuals or dispose of them with the household rubbish.

Developing Your Hobby

**Learning more and showing
and breeding goldfish**

*As you gain in experience and enjoyment of keeping goldfish,
you may want to progress to keeping some of the more 'difficult'
fancy varieties or to establishing a second or larger aquarium.
You may even decide to try exhibiting your goldfish or breeding a
pair and raising their fry. You will almost certainly want to make
contact with others who share your hobby.*

Joining a society

You can, of course, learn lots more about goldfish by reading other books, subscribing to fishkeeping magazines, talking to your local aquatic dealer or surfing the Internet. One of the best ways of gaining access to a wealth of information about keeping goldfish, however, is to join one of the many goldfish societies. Joining one will put you in touch with other, often more experienced, fishkeepers and will keep you up to date with information on new varieties and their availability and showing fish.

Goldfish shows

Some societies will include sections in their shows for pet goldfish, where the main criteria by which the fish are judged are good health, colour and body shape. For fish breeders and serious hobbyists, however, rearing and exhibiting would-be champion goldfish is a much more challenging undertaking. Successfully rearing goldfish to produce high-quality specimens with the desirable attributes for the particular variety takes dedication and patience. For serious goldfish breeders, the mark of success lies in showing fancy goldfish.

These goldfish are in their show tanks after judging. The labels on the tanks indicate the position achieved and points scored.

SHOW STANDARDS

All goldfish varieties are judged by set standards in five categories: body, fins, colour, special characteristics, and condition and deportment. Each category can earn 20 points, with a possible total of 100, but with marks deducted for faults.

The dorsal fin is single and being held erect, which would gain this fish extra points.

The standards specify the ideal proportion of tail and body length and minimum length of body.

Body depth should be in a certain proportion to length – in fantails at least three-fifths of the body length.

Fin shape is a key factor – in fantails the caudal fin should be divided and forked.

The colour pattern should be similar on both sides of the body. The good colour pattern of this fish is clearly visible when viewed from above.

Breeding Goldfish – and caring for fry

Breeding goldfish is not a task for beginners to fishkeeping. Not only do you need space for a nursery tank in which to raise the babies (and a home for the youngsters that survive), but the eggs and hatchlings need a lot of care.

The goldfish breeding cycle

Goldfish don't breed until they are mature – about two years old. In the breeding season, females will grow plumper and males will develop breeding tubercles (round white spots) on their heads, gill covers and pectoral fins. Males will chase females for several days before spawning (egg-laying) occurs. Once the eggs are laid, there is no parental care – indeed the parent goldfish will often eat their young.

Encouraging breeding

Place two males and one female in the largest possible tank, equipped with a simple sponge filter. Create an artificial summertime in the aquarium to encourage breeding by increasing the hours of

MAKING A SPAWNING MOP

In the aquarium, eggs can adhere to a spawning mop. Wind green nylon wool about 30 times around a book, then wrap another length of wool, about 20cm (8in) long, under the strands and secure with a tight knot. Cut the wool strands at the opposite point to your knot. Wash the mop in warm water before its first use (and before reusing it). Attach the long ends to a cork to keep the mop at the water surface.

Note the tubercles on the gill covers of this male Redcap Oranda (left). The female will lay her eggs in the dense vegetation.

lighting, carrying out daily 20% water changes and adding live or frozen food, such as brineshrimp, to the diet. The fish should spawn within a few days. Once they have done so, remove the parent fish to the main aquarium to prevent them eating the eggs and fry.

Caring for the fry

The eggs will hatch in about four to five days and the newly hatched fry will look like tiny hairs attached to the spawning mop at first. For the first few days they don't need feeding, as they are still absorbing food from their yolk sacs. When they swim away from the mops, they need special fry food consisting of microscopic organisms and algae. They will need feeding regularly but take particular care to remove uneaten food and monitor water quality daily.

Assuming they are in no danger of being eaten by larger, adult goldfish, the babies can be removed to the main aquarium as soon as they reach about 2cm (¾in) long, which may take as little as six weeks. However, be aware that at this size they may still be vulnerable to damage from strong filter intakes, so check the equipment you are using.

These nine-week-old Red Metallic Ranchus will still need heavy feeding.

THE BREEDING TANK

Do not disturb the mops after spawning to allow the eggs to develop.

Heat the aquarium temperature to slightly higher than usual: 20°C (68°F).

Use a simple sponge filter as larvae or fry could be sucked into filter mechanisms.

Reduce the water depth to 15cm (6in) for the tiny fry once the fish have spawned.

Further Information

RECOMMENDED BOOKS

Goldfish: A Complete Pet Owner's Manual
Ostrow, Marshall (Barron's, 1995)
Caring For Your Pet Goldfish
Sands, Dr David (Interpet Publishing, 1996)
Guide to Fancy Goldfish Andrews, Dr Chris
(Interpet Publishing, 1996)
Pet Owner's Guide to the Goldfish
Windsor, Steve (Ringpress Books, 1996)
Getting to Know Your Goldfish
Page, Gill (Interpet Publishing, 2001)
An Essential Guide to Keeping Goldfish
Brewster, Bernice (Interpet Publishing, 2003)
Gold Medal Guide: Golden Tips For Keeping
Your First Goldfish O'Neill, Amanda
(Interpet Publishing, 2004)

CLUBS

The Goldfish Society of America, P.O. Box
551373, Fort Lauderdale, FL 33555, USA
The Goldfish Society of Great Britain,
62 Balstonia Drive, Stanford le Hope,
Essex, SS17 8HX, UK.

RECOMMENDED WEBSITES

http://www.goldfishinfo.com
http://www.petlibrary.com/goldfish/goldfish.html
http://kokosgoldfish.com
http://www.bristol-aquarists.org.uk

PICTURE CREDITS

The majority of the pictures
in this book were taken by
Geoffrey Rogers and Neil
Sutherland and are the
copyright of Interpet
Publishing. Those on the
following pages were supplied
by and are the copyright of
www.photomax.org.uk:
13 (bottom right), 15 (top),
17 (bottom), 18 (right).